ANIMALS
That Make a Difference!

Birds

Ashley Lee

Explore other books at:
WWW.ENGAGEBOOKS.COM

VANCOUVER, B.C.

WWW.ENGAGEBOOKS.COM

Birds: Level 1
Animals That Make a Difference!
Lee, Ashley 1995 –
Text © 2021 Engage Books

Edited by: A.R. Roumanis
and Lauren Dick

Text set in Arial Regular.
Chapter headings set in Arial Black.

FIRST EDITION / FIRST PRINTING

LIBRARY AND ARCHIVES CANADA CATALOGUING IN PUBLICATION

Title: Animals That Make a Difference: Birds Level 1
Names: Lee, Ashley, author.

Identifiers: Canadiana (print) 20200309749 | Canadiana (ebook) 20200309757
ISBN 978-1-77437-702-4 (hardcover)
ISBN 978-1-77437-703-1 (softcover)
ISBN 978-1-77437-704-8 (pdf)
ISBN 978-1-77437-705-5 (epub)
ISBN 978-1-77437-706-2 (kindle)

Subjects:
LCSH: Birds—Juvenile literature
LCSH: Human-animal relationships—Juvenile literature

Classification: LCC RA644.C68 R682 2020 | DDC J614.5/92—DC23

Contents

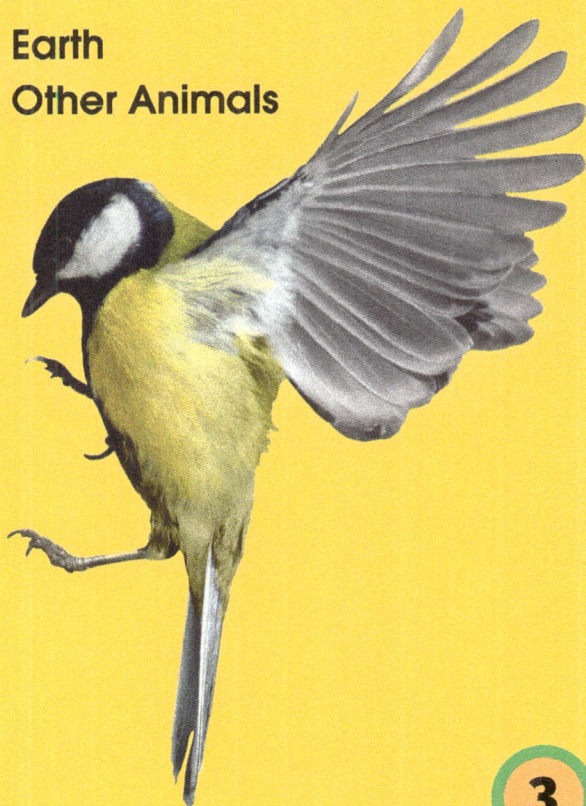

What Are Birds?

Birds are animals with feathers and wings.

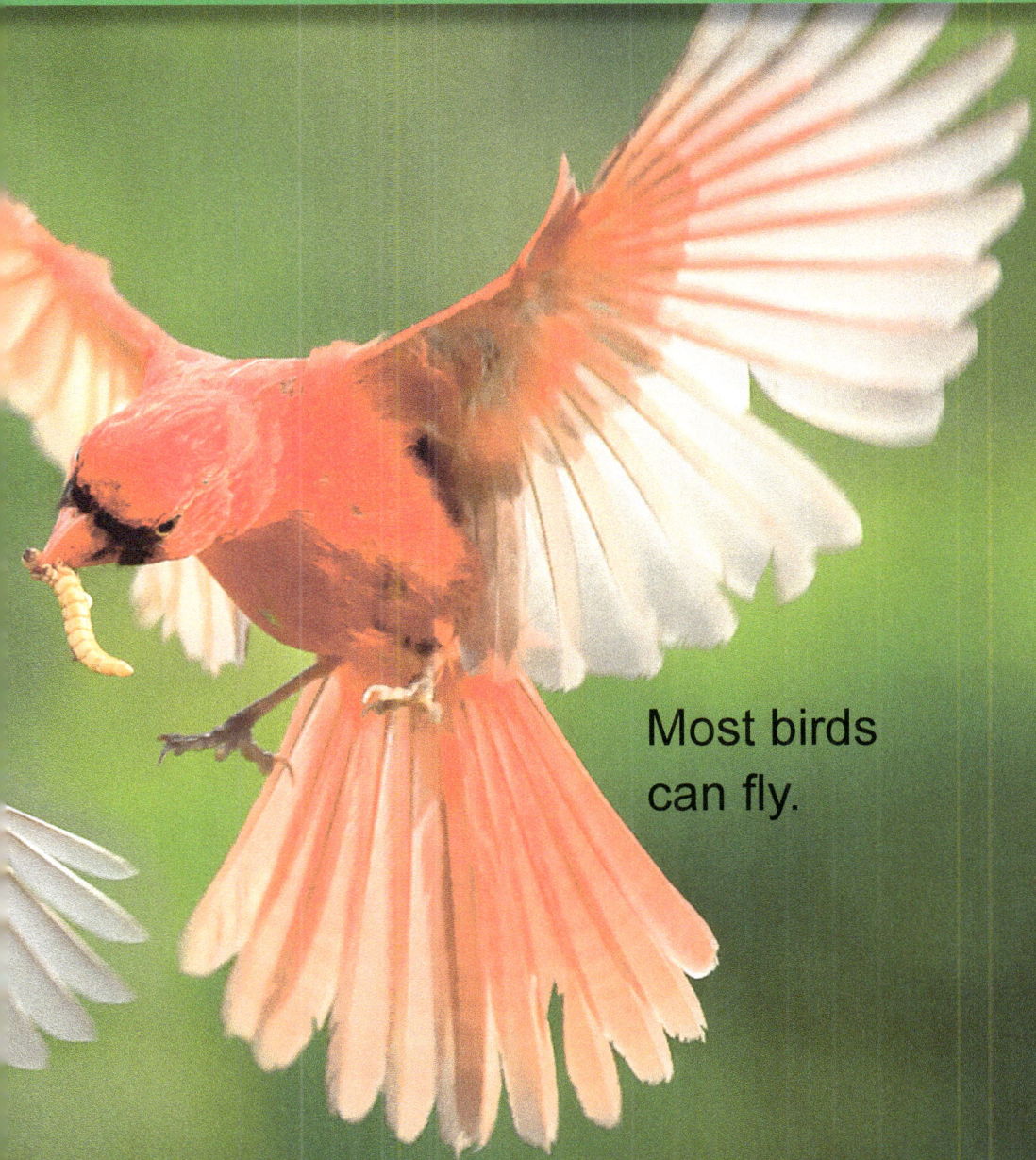

Most birds
can fly.

What Do Birds Look Like?

The smallest birds are
bee hummingbirds.
They are only 2.4 inches
(6 centimeters) long.
The largest birds are
ostriches. They
can be up to 9 feet
(2.7 meters) tall.

Birds have two
wings. They are
covered in feathers.

Birds have
a hard nose
and mouth
called a beak.

Birds have
sharp nails
called claws.

Where Do Birds Live?

Birds live all over the world. They sleep in trees, logs, or under bushes.

Kiwi birds are only found in New Zealand. Ceylon magpies live in Sri Lanka. Madagascar jacunas live on the coast of Madagascar.

Arctic Ocean

Madagascar

Europe

Asia

Sri Lanka

Africa

Pacific Ocean

Atlantic Ocean

Australia

New Zealand

Southern Ocean

Antarctica

0   2,000 miles

0   4,000 kilometers

N

Legend

☐ Land

☐ Ocean

What Do Birds Eat?

Birds eat many different foods. Some birds eat seeds, fruit, or insects.

Larger birds
will eat fish or
small animals.

How Do Birds Talk to Each Other?

Birds use special calls to find other birds, warn other birds of danger, or scare other animals away.

Some male birds do special dances to impress female birds.

Bird Life Cycle

Most female birds lay eggs in nests.

They sit on their eggs to keep them warm.

14

Most baby birds hatch after 10 to 21 days.
They usually leave home after a few weeks.

Some birds live longer than others. Most
finches live for 5 to 10 years. The Laysan
albatross can live for more than 60 years.

Curious Facts About Birds

Some birds fly to areas with warmer weather in the winter. This is called migration.

Owls cannot move their eyes. Instead they can turn their heads in almost a complete circle.

Parrots and ravens can learn to talk.

People once used pigeons to carry messages across long distances.

Birds have hollow bones. They are filled with pockets of air.

Over time, dinosaurs with feathers turned into birds.

Kinds of Birds

There are more than 10,000 different kinds of birds. All birds walk on two legs. Chickens are the most common kind of bird.

Quetzal birds are brightly colored. Some quetzals have tails that are longer than their bodies.

Penguins cannot fly. They use their wings to help them swim underwater.

Emus can run up to 30 miles (50 kilometers) per hour.

How Birds Help Earth

Birds eat many seeds. These seeds come out in their poop. Bird poop helps the seeds grow into new plants.

Some birds help plants make new seeds. They bring pollen from male plants to female plants. The female plants can then make seeds. This is called pollination.

How Birds Help Other Animals

Some birds eat bugs that harm other animals.

Oxpeckers sit on the backs of zebras, giraffes, and buffalo. They eat bugs called ticks that eat other animals' blood.

How Birds Help Humans

Veery birds will leave an area if a hurricane is on the way. Hurricanes are strong storms that create strong winds and heavy rain.

Scientists study veeries so they know when a bad hurricane is going to hit an area.

Birds in Danger

Some birds have gone extinct. This means there are no more of them left.

The Alagoas foliage-gleaner became extinct in 2018. People destroyed their forests in Brazil.

Some birds are endangered.
This means they may soon
go extinct.

The kakapo is also
called the owl parrot.
They cannot fly and
are an easy meal for
other hungry animals.

How To Help Birds

Many birds get trapped in pieces of garbage. They also try to eat garbage. This can hurt them.

Many people are organizing garbage clean-ups in their neighbourhoods. This can help keep birds safe.

Quiz

Test your knowledge of birds by answering the following questions. The questions are based on what you have read in this book. The answers are listed on the bottom of the next page.

1 Where do birds sleep?

2 What do some male birds do to impress female birds?

3 Why do most female birds sit on their eggs?

4 What two birds can learn to talk?

5 What is the most common kind of bird?

6 What do oxpeckers eat?

Explore other books in the Animals That Make a Difference series.

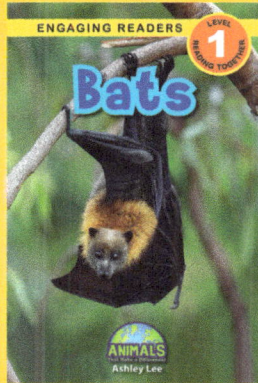

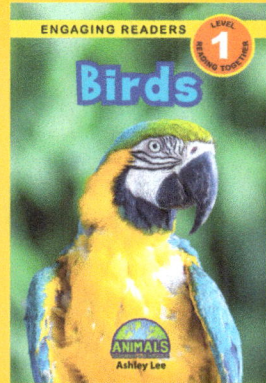

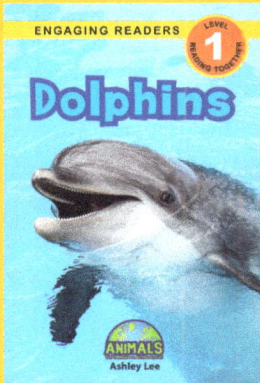

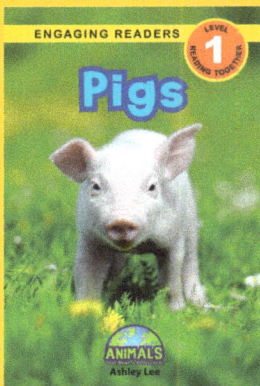

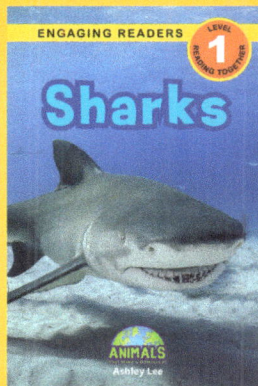

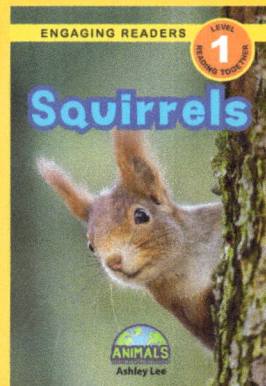

ENGAGING READERS — LEVEL 1 — READING TOGETHER
Bees
ANIMALS
Jared Siemens

ENGAGING READERS — LEVEL 1 — READING TOGETHER
Bats
ANIMALS
Ashley Lee

ENGAGING READERS — LEVEL 1 — READING TOGETHER
Birds
ANIMALS
Ashley Lee

ENGAGING READERS — LEVEL 1 — READING TOGETHER
Dolphins
ANIMALS
Ashley Lee

ENGAGING READERS — LEVEL 1 — READING TOGETHER
Horses
ANIMALS
Ashley Lee

ENGAGING READERS — LEVEL 1 — READING TOGETHER
Ladybugs
ANIMALS
Ashley Lee

ENGAGING READERS — LEVEL 1 — READING TOGETHER
Pigs
ANIMALS
Ashley Lee

ENGAGING READERS — LEVEL 1 — READING TOGETHER
Sharks
ANIMALS
Ashley Lee

ENGAGING READERS — LEVEL 1 — READING TOGETHER
Squirrels
ANIMALS
Ashley Lee

Visit www.engagebooks.com to explore more Engaging Readers.

Answers:
1. In trees, logs, or bushes 2. Special dances 3. To keep them warm 4. Parrots and ravens 5. Chickens 6. Ticks

31

www.ingramcontent.com/pod-product-compliance
Lightning Source LLC
Chambersburg PA
CBHW051235020426
42331CB00016B/3384